ÁSÍYIH KHÁNUM
THE MOST EXALTED LEAF
entitled Navváb

MONUMENTS OF ÁSÍYIH KHÁNUM,
ENTITLED NAVVÁB, AND OF MÍRZÁ MIHDÍ,
THE PUREST BRANCH

ÁSÍYIH KHÁNUM
The Most Exalted Leaf
entitled Navváb

by

BAHARIEH ROUHANI MA'ANI

GEORGE RONALD
OXFORD

GEORGE RONALD, *Publisher*
Oxford
www.grbooks.com

© BAHARIEH ROUHANI MA'ANI 1993
All Rights Reserved

First published in hardcover 1993
Softcover edition 2008

ISBN 978-0-85398-353-4 HC
ISBN 978-0-85398-354-5 SC

*A catalogue record for this book is available
from the British Library*

CONTENTS

INTRODUCTION   I

ÁSÍYIH K͟HÁNUM, THE MOST EXALTED LEAF
     ENTITLED NAVVÁB   7

REFERENCES   75

Enlarge the place of thy tent, and let them stretch forth the curtains of thine habitations: spare not, lengthen thy cords, and strengthen thy stakes; For thou shalt break forth on the right hand and on the left; and thy seed shall inherit the Gentiles, and make the desolate cities to be inhabited . . . For thy Maker is thine husband, the Lord of hosts is his name; and thy Redeemer the Holy One of Israel; the God of the whole earth shall he be called.

ISAIAH[1]

INTRODUCTION

This essay is about Ásíyih Khánum, the faithful wife of Bahá'u'lláh, the one whom God 'hath made . . . to be His companion in every one of His worlds, and hath nourished thee . . . with His meeting and presence, so long as His Name, and His Remembrance, and His Kingdom, and His Empire shall endure.'[2]

Although 'God hath so exalted' Ásíyih Khánum that, according to Bahá'u'lláh, 'all honour and glory circled around'[3] her, the information which has been passed on to us about her is very scanty. We have voluminous books written about outstanding believers in the Faith, but we do not have basic information about two of the most important women in the life of the Supreme Manifestation of God: His mother, the one who bore Him, gave birth to Him, and raised Him, and 'the one whom God created to arise and serve His own Self, and the Manifestation of His Cause . . .', the one who 'didst turn with [her] whole being unto Him, at a time when His servants and handmaidens had turned away from His Face . . .'⁴, His wife, Ásíyih Khánum.

There are reasons for the painful lack of documentation about these remarkable women in our Faith. To discuss such reasons in full would require an analysis of the social and religious conditions of Iran when it was chosen to become the Cradle of a new World Faith. In brief, the record of the early history of the Bahá'í Faith in Iran is influenced by nineteenth-century Islamic traditions and practices. Although the treatment of women in religious history in the early stages of the Muḥammadan Dispensation was far more equitable,* by the time of the revelation of the Báb and Bahá'u'lláh in the middle of the nineteenth century women had lost their standing in society, had very little apparent influence on events that took place outside their

---

* Absence of arbitrary religious and traditional restrictions enabled the seventh-century historians to provide biographical data about women, including those closely related to Muḥammad. As a result we know who His mother was and when and where she died. We know the particulars of His foster mother. A great deal is known about Khadíjih, His first wife, and about her support for Muḥammad when He first received revelation from God. We have much information about Muḥammad and Khadíjih's daughter, Fáṭimih, even though she died when she was only eighteen. We also know the particulars of several women Muḥammad married. Moreover, the freedom the women enjoyed at the beginning of Islám made it possible for Áyishih, Muḥammad's favourite wife after Khadíjih had died, to personally go to war, during the War of the Camel, against Imám 'Alí. These facts are all recorded in the history of Islám.

homes, and unless they soared above all the barriers that society had placed in the way of their emancipation and won conspicuous and extraordinary achievements, were ignored by historians of the time.

Lack of education, a privilege generally open only to the men, had pushed women completely out of the arena of national and local affairs. The clergy controlled everything; their biased views of women went unchallenged. Their distorted understanding of the laws of the Qur'án, which they had assumed the right to interpret, had made of women an object of pleasure which men owned and treated as they pleased. A woman's 'honour' required that she remain as obscure as possible, and men did everything to ensure that the women of their household remained 'honourable'. Their absence from the local and national scene, their inability to read and grasp the significance of the events which shaped and controlled their destiny, their acceptance without question of clerical pronouncements, and their general obscurity made them an unknown entity for historians to deal with. Since the historians were all men, who could not trespass the limits imposed upon them by society, they considered in their histories only those women about whom information was readily available. For this reason we have ample information about a personality like Ṭáhirih who tore down all the traditional barriers and emerged as a prodigy. Her acts were so extraordinary, conspicuous, and bold that no historian could ignore them. But those very acts invoked the wrath of her family and the society in which she lived. She laid down her life for her high ideals and for living up to them.

The dearth of authentic information about Ásíyih Khánum is rooted in the pathetic situation of women in countries under Islamic rule and influence in the nineteenth century. Iran was one such country. The early historians of the Bahá'í Faith did not consider it appropriate, partly out of respect for the head of the household, and partly in order to honour the existing trend, to seek information about women. Such considerations were particularly observed with regard to female members of the Holy Family. When it was necessary to make mention of such women, they avoided identifying them by their names, instead referring to them by their relationship to a man of renown. Ásíyih Khánum, for example, is mentioned in two places in *The Dawn-Breakers* as 'Varaqatu'l-'Ulyá', the title bestowed upon her by Bahá'u'lláh meaning 'the Most Exalted Leaf', and as the mother of the Greatest Branch.* These two references will be discussed in more detail later. Not until recent years in the history of the Faith did historians start using the name 'Navváb' and provide such little information about her as was available.

---

* 'Abdu'l-Bahá

The purpose of this essay is to make available to the reader whatever information has been possible to gather about a personage whose 'Maker' has been her 'husband, the Lord of hosts', and whose monument along with those of her daughter* and martyred son† is the focal point of the Arc on Mount Carmel, around which the international institutions of the Faith are housed.

---

* Bahá'íyyih K͟hánum, entitled the Greatest Holy Leaf
† Mírzá Mihdí, entitled the Purest Branch

Ásíyih Khánum's earthly life, which covered a span of between sixty and sixty-five years, can be divided into four distinct periods: her childhood and girlhood; her marriage to Bahá'u'lláh and the years immediately following; her life after Bahá'u'lláh embraced the Cause of the Báb; and the years when she accompanied Bahá'u'lláh into exile.

Ásíyih Khánum Before Her Marriage to Bahá'u'lláh

No information is available about Ásíyih Khánum's life from the time she was born until she married Bahá'u'lláh. We do not even have the date of her birth; her tombstone bears only the date of her death. Her date of birth, as was the custom of the time, had probably been recorded inside the cover of the Qur'án or another book held dear by the family. This information was never looked up or inquired about, and is now lost to posterity. None of the history books contain it.

Ásíyih Khánum's father was Mírzá Ismá'íl Vazír-i-Yálrúdí. The word 'vazír' means 'minister' in

Persian, and it indicates that he had an important government position in Yálrúd, a village in the District of Núr. Her mother's name is not mentioned in any of the available historical sources. Mírzá Ismá'íl was also known as Navváb; a title of honour meaning deputy. His daughter, Ásíyih, was called Navvábih, which is the feminine and diminutive form of Navváb. The title indicates that from childhood she evinced signs of nobility and was considered 'the secret essence of [her] sire'. Bahá'u'lláh later referred to her in His Tablets as Navváb, a masculine title, and used the masculine pronoun when referring to her in the third person singular. This is the title by which she is known by the Bahá'ís. She also became known, after her exile, as 'Buyúk Khánum', a Turkish title of honour meaning 'great'. In the Bahá'í International Archives there is a cupboard containing a few items belonging to 'Buyúk Khánum'.

In some of His Writings 'Abdu'l-Bahá has referred to His mother's name. In a Tablet addressed to a believer in the United States, He confirms that Ásíyih was the name of His mother:

The name Aseyeh is accepted in the Threshold of Oneness, for the daughter of Pharaoh had this name, who, when (Moses) the Light of Guidance dawned, became confirmed by the Merciful One, left the court of Pharaoh with its grandeur and sovereignty and became perfumed with the fragrances of holiness. Then she assisted in the service of His Holiness (Moses) – upon him be peace! Also, Aseyeh was the name of my mother.[5]

In another Tablet He says:

That blessed name which thou hast asked to remain with thee forever and become the cause of spiritual progress – that name is 'Aseyeh', which is the name of the mother of 'Abdu'l-Bahá. I give the blessed name to thee. Be therefore in the utmost joy and happiness, and be engaged in all gladness and attraction (or ecstasy) for thou hast become the object of such a favour.[6]

Ásíyih Khánum's life as a girl of tender age, growing up in her parents' home in Yálrúd, assumed significance when her brother Mírzá Maḥmúd was joined in wedlock with Sárih Khánum, Bahá'u'lláh's eldest sister. Sárih Khánum seems to have been the first person to recognize the extraordinary spiritual qualities and physical beauty of the young woman whose brother she had married. Her close association with Ásíyih Khánum increased her admiration for her to the point that she desired her marriage to Bahá'u'lláh, a brother she loved dearly and served devotedly. Bahá'í history credits Sárih Khánum with arranging the marriage of Bahá'u'lláh to Ásíyih Khánum.

The custom of the time did not allow young men and women who were eligible for marriage to choose their partners in life. It was generally the man's family, and particularly his mother or sister, who were responsible for choosing a suitable wife for him. If the choice was satisfactory, negotiations and arrangements would follow. The family of the woman had the right to approve or disapprove the proposition put to them. Their approval, usually given after a lengthy process of negotiations, made it possible for the arrangements to proceed. As men and women married very young in those days, the families had to support them initially until they had their independent means of livelihood. This factor was taken into consideration when negotiations for marriage were in process. Although marriage arrangements and customs were not uniform everywhere in Iran, the following was more or less the norm.

The parents of the bride usually provided 'Jaház' or 'Jahízíyyih' (a form of dowry) consisting, in accordance with the wealth of the family, of furnishing for a house (particularly soft furnishings such as drapery and linen), dinner and tea sets, utensils, silverware, all kinds of accessories, servants and maidservants, often slaves who lived more or less as members of the family. The parents of the groom provided the cost of the wedding, very elaborate in those days, and 'Mahr' or 'Mahríyyih' (dowry – a mutually agreed amount – usually considerable). The dowry did not have to be paid in cash; it was often in the form of the transfer of a title deed or a promissory note. If the marriage ceremony and the reception were not combined, the ceremony usually took place in the bride's family house and the expenses defrayed by her parents. The wedding reception and the expenditures involved were the responsibility of the groom's parents.

Ásíyih Khánum's Marriage to Bahá'u'lláh

According to all Bahá'í historical sources, Ásíyih Khánum married as soon as she reached the age of maturity. However, we do not know her actual age at the time of her marriage. The author of *Akhtarán-i-Tábán*, Furúgh Arbáb, tells us that she was fifteen years old when she married,[7] but there does not appear to be any evidence for this. In addition, the age of maturity for girls in Islam is nine, and it was quite common in nineteenth-century Iran for girls to marry when they reached their ninth birthday. Since Ásíyih Khánum married according to Islamic law, it is more reasonable to assume that she was any age between nine and fifteen. If we presume that she was fifteen when she married Bahá'u'lláh, the date of her birth can be said to have been around 1236 AH (about 1820 AD), because the known date of her marriage is Jamádíyu'th-Thání 1251 AH (about October 1835 AD). On the basis of this calculation, she would have been three years younger than Bahá'u'lláh, Who was eighteen years old when He married Ásíyih Khánum. As mentioned before, this is very uncertain and there is no evidence to indicate the accuracy of such a presumption. According to Bahá'íyyih Khánum, the Greatest Holy Leaf, her mother married her father 'when she was very young'.[8]

The marriage of Sárih Khánum,* Bahá'u'lláh's sister, with Mírzá Mahmúd, which took place in 1832 when Bahá'u'lláh was fifteen years old, united the families of Mírzá Buzurg of Tákur† and Mírzá Ismá'íl of Yálrúd†. Ásíyih Khánum was probably under ten at that time. Whether the marriage of Sárih Khánum and Mírzá Mahmúd, and the visits that Bahá'u'lláh made to Yálrúd before and after His sister's marriage, provided any opportunity for Him and Ásíyih Khánum to see each other prior to their marriage is a matter left to the imagination of the reader.

Ásíyih Khánum, as attested by her Marriage Certificate‡ and remarked by her daughter, Bahá'íyyih Khánum, possessed wonderful human attributes and perfections. When Mírzá Buzurg and Khadíjih Khánum§ acceded to Sárih Khánum's

---

* Sárih Khánum, who was of the same mother and father as Bahá'u'lláh, was utterly devoted to Him. Her allegiance to Bahá'u'lláh caused her untold hardships and sufferings. In a Tablet revealed after her passing Bahá'u'lláh remembers her affectionately and says there is as much reward in visiting her grave as there is in visiting Him.
† Two villages in the District of Núr
‡ The Marriage Certificate of Bahá'u'lláh and Ásíyih Khánum has been published in the original language in *Iqlím-i-Núr* by Muhammad-'Alí Malik Khusrawví. The original has been framed and placed in the International Archives Building.
§ Bahá'u'lláh's mother

request, in accordance with the customs of the time, they would have approached the parents of Ásíyih Khánum to seek their approval for the marriage, unless Sárih Khánum had already prepared the ground. In any case, acquiring consent for the marriage from the parties concerned does not seem to have been problematic. Already related to each other by the marriage of their older children, the families were well acquainted; they came from the same region of Núr; they were prominent, wealthy, and renowned.

The preparations for the wedding in the year 1835 AD were elaborate. The Marriage Certificate specifies the enormity of the dowry which included two maidservants, one servant, a considerable sum of money and a large piece of property. The size of Ásíyih Khánum's 'Jaház' – the dowry provided by her parents – was such that, according to the spoken chronicle of her daughter Bahá'íyyih Khánum, 'forty mules were loaded with her possessions when she came to her husband's home . . . For six months before the marriage a jeweller worked at her home, preparing jewellery – even the buttons of her garments were of gold, set with precious stones.'[9]

It should be mentioned here that the Islamic law of inheritance affords the female offspring of the deceased father only half of what his male offspring inherit. It is to compensate for this inequity that the female offspring are given at the time of their marriage as much as their parents can afford in the form of Jaház. As we will see, the remnants of Ásíyih Khánum's Jaház helped later to provide some means of sustenance and relief to the family when Bahá'u'lláh had been divested of His earthly belongings and banished from Iran.

All that is known of Ásíyih Khánum's life as a young married woman is that she lived sometimes in Ṭihrán; at other times in Tákur. She undoubtedly visited Yálrúd as well, and spent time with her family there. According to H.M. Balyuzi, 'Whenever He returned to His home in Tákur, Bahá'u'lláh would usually stop for a while in Yálrúd, and here He would visit the mujtahid,* who was distantly related to His family.'[10] Since his faithful sister, Sárih Khánum, and Ásíyih Khánum's family lived in Yálrúd, Ásíyih Khánum no doubt accompanied Bahá'u'lláh on many such journeys. And as the means of travel was by mule, whenever she undertook trips to Yálrúd and Tákur she probably stayed for a considerable time.

The course of Ásíyih Khánum's life during the first nine years of her marriage was, compared with the latter years, smooth and uneventful. As a young woman of noble lineage married to a renowned nobleman, she was provided with the

---

* The name of this mujtahid was Mírzá Taqí, known as 'Allámiy-i-Núrí. He is believed to have married Bahá'u'lláh's cousin Fáṭimih towards the end of his life. No children were born of this marriage. He died in 1843–44, before the Báb declared His mission. Bahá'u'lláh married Fáṭimih Khánum in 1849.

needs of a comfortable life. Her time must have, therefore, been spent more in association with the members of the family which, in those days, was much more closely knit together than it is now. She also engaged in charitable pursuits. According to Bahá'íyyih Khánum:

. . . in the early years of their married life, they, my father and mother, took part as little as possible in State functions, social ceremonies, and the luxurious habits of ordinary highly-placed and wealthy families in the land of Persia; she, and her noble-hearted husband, counted these worldly pleasures meaningless, and preferred rather to occupy themselves in caring for the poor, and for all who were unhappy, or in trouble.

From our doors nobody was ever turned away; the hospitable board was spread for all comers.

Constantly the poor women came to my mother, to whom they poured out their various stories of woe, to be comforted and consoled by her loving helpfulness.

Whilst the people called my father 'The Father of the Poor', they spoke of my mother as 'The Mother of Consolation', though, naturally, only the women and little children ever looked upon her face unveiled.[11]

During this period Ásíyih Khánum bore three children. The first two, a boy by the name of Kázim, and a girl (name unknown) died in infancy. Her later children were born about two years apart, so if this pattern prevailed earlier too, her first child would have been born about 1839–40. If so, it may add to the likelihood of her extreme youth at the time of her marriage in 1835.

Five years after her marriage, in 1840, Bahá'u'lláh's father Mírzá Buzurg, passed away. During the later years of his life Mírzá Buzurg's fortunes had suffered a setback and he had lost almost everything. He was survived by several wives and children, some of them under age. Bahá'u'lláh rented a house near the gate of Shimírán in Ṭihrán, where His mother, stepmothers, sisters and brothers lived under his care. Considering the lifestyle of traditional Iranian families at the time, this change must have been readily accepted by Ásíyih Khánum; she quickly adapted to the new requirements of her life as the wife of a senior member of the family who, after the passing of His father, had shouldered responsibility for his unprotected survivors. There is no mention of Bahá'u'lláh and Ásíyih Khánum having any living children by then. Their first child had probably been born and passed away before this development. Ásíyih Khánum, although young in age, shared by virtue of her position the responsibility of caring and providing for this large family, and no doubt had the respect and appreciation of those under Bahá'u'lláh's care. Her gentle and loving disposition, her captivating demeanour and selfless attitude facilitated the creation of the atmosphere and situation desirable in such circumstances.

THE MOST EXALTED LEAF

Bahá'u'lláh and Ásíyih Khánum's third child was born on 22 May 1844. His birth coincided with the night the Báb declared His Mission in Shíráz. He was named 'Abbás after His grandfather. This child survived; he would in the future adopt 'Abdu'l-Bahá (Servant of Bahá) as His title. At the age of ten, before Bahá'u'lláh declared His Mission in Baghdad, He would recognize His station and consecrate His life to the service of His Cause. He would share all His Father's exiles and represent Him at meetings with government officials and dignitaries. He would be named, in a document in the handwriting of Bahá'u'lláh, as His successor and the Centre of His Covenant. In the latter part of His life He would travel extensively in the countries of Europe and North America and promulgate the principles of His Father's Faith.

Ásíyih Khánum's joy was complete as she saw him grow and become stronger day by day. He was still in his infancy when the Báb's envoy arrived in Ṭihrán. The family was then living in the house near the gate of Shimírán situated near the School of Mírzá Ṣáliḥ known as Madrisih of Páy-i-Minár, where Mullá Ḥusayn, the Báb's envoy, was staying. It was in this Madrisih that Mullá Ḥusayn met Mullá Muḥammad-i-Núrí, who led him to Bahá'u'lláh, the Hidden Secret the Báb had sent him to Ṭihrán to find, and to Whom he was to deliver a message on His behalf. Bahá'u'lláh accepted the Báb as the promised Qá'im of Islam and arose to promote His Cause.

Ásíyih Khánum's Life After Bahá'u'lláh Embraced the Cause of the Báb

Bahá'u'lláh accepted the Mission of the Báb soon after 'Abdu'l-Bahá's birth. As He grew older, Bahá'u'lláh's involvement with the new Faith became more intense, and Ásíyih Khánum had to cope not only with the demands of motherhood, but adjust to the rapid changes which were taking place around her. Bahá'u'lláh's house became the focal centre of the activities of the followers of the nascent Faith in Ṭihrán, and Ásíyih Khánum, the lady of the household, was their gracious and loving hostess and had to see to their needs and comfort in the way desired by Bahá'u'lláh. Her life then underwent the same drastic change which affected all those who accepted the Revelation of the Báb. The conditions of the time did not allow her to associate with her Husband's guests, who were generally men, or participate in the meetings they held. But she could, from her private parlour, witness the movements of the guests and follow the developments.* She must have been fully aware of

---

* Oriental houses in the olden days were comprised of two sections: the Andarún or the inner section which remained beyond the reach of men who were not immediate members of the family; and the Bírúní or outer section, where male guests were received and entertained. The setting up of the two sections of the house was such that women from behind curtains in their quarters could see what was going on in the Bírúní, but not vice versa.

the many events that were being shaped. Unfortunately, no details are available to indicate the degree of her knowledge, involvement and reaction, which would have provided a sure basis for an historical description and analysis. In the absence of such details, one has to rely upon scraps of evidence and draw conclusions.

During this time when Ásíyih Khánum was in Ṭihrán and observed the frequent comings and goings of the Bábís, she must have met and associated closely with prominent female believers such as Ṭáhirih and Varaqatu'l-Firdaws. These two women were Bahá'u'lláh's house guests for a while. Ṭáhirih lived in Bahá'u'lláh's house after she was rescued, at His behest, from imprisonment in Qazvín. No doubt she used the 'Andarúní' (the inner section) of the house. The story describing Ṭáhirih addressing her fellow-believers gathered in the 'Bírúní' (the outer section) of the house from behind a curtain helps us to gain intriguing insights into some aspects of Ásíyih Khánum's life which have remained thus far obscure. 'Abdu'l-Bahá relates in *Memorials of the Faithful* the circumstances of a visit paid by Vaḥíd to Ṭáhirih, while the latter was staying in the home of Bahá'u'lláh in Ṭihrán. Ṭáhirih, He writes:

was listening from behind the veil to the utterances of Vaḥíd, who was discoursing with fervour and eloquence on the signs and verses that bore witness to the advent of the new Manifestation. I was then a child and was sitting on her lap, as she followed the recital of the remarkable testimonies which flowed ceaselessly from the lips of that learned man. I well remember how she suddenly interrupted him and, raising her voice, vehemently declared: 'O Yaḥyá! Let deeds, not words, testify to thy faith, if thou art a man of true learning . . .'[12]

As the story is about the early years of 'Abdu'l-Bahá's childhood, it must have occurred in His mother's residence. This is confirmed by the story related by 'Abdu'l-Bahá when He was in London. The story has been recorded by Lady Blomfield. It reads:

He, being a little boy, was sitting on the knee of Qurratu'l-'Ayn, who was in the private parlour of His mother, Ásíyih Khánum; the door of this room being open, they could hear, from behind the curtain, the voice of Siyyid Yaḥyáy-i-Dárábí, who was talking . . . [13]

Bíbí Kúchak, whom Bahá'u'lláh entitled Varaqatu'l-Firdaws (Leaf of Paradise) had been a Shaykhí; she and her mother (sister and mother of Mullá Ḥusayn), attended the classes of Siyyid Káẓim-i-Rashtí in Karbilá. They recognized the station of the Báb through Ṭáhirih. Varaqatu'l-Firdaws later married Shaykh Abú Turáb-i-Ishtihárdı, whom Bahá'u'lláh appointed to 'watch

THE MOST EXALTED LEAF

over' Ṭáhirih 'and ensure her protection and safety' in Núr, after the incident in Níyálá.[14] It was probably because of his wife's intimacy with Ṭáhirih that he was chosen for this service. Ásíyih Khánum may have been in Núr when Bahá'u'lláh arrived there, accompanied by Ṭáhirih and her attendant.

Varaqatu'l-Firdaws became a prominent Bábí and a renowned teacher of the Faith. Ishráq-Khávarí says she was with Ṭáhirih in Baghdad, Hamadán, and other places; she was in Bahá'u'lláh's house in Ṭihrán; she attained His presence several times; and was a close associate of Bahá'u'lláh's wife, Ásíyih Khánum. After the Shaykh Ṭabarsí upheaval, she accompanied her mother to Bushrúyih, their native land, and became a target for intense persecution. She spent the last years of her life in 'Ishqábád serving the Faith. Bahá'u'lláh has revealed in her honour a Tablet of Visitation for Mullá Ḥusayn and the martyrs of Shaykh Ṭabarsí.

Ásíyih Khánum's strong intuition, her utter devotion to Bahá'u'lláh, her observation of the leading role her Husband played in guiding and inspiring the Bábís, coupled with her close association with these prominent Bábí figures who were aware of Bahá'u'lláh's exalted station, must have confirmed her in His glorious destiny. It is inconceivable that a person of Ásíyih Khánum's spiritual endowments would have remained untouched by all the happenings which took place around her.

ÁSÍYIH KHÁNUM

Indeed, the fact that she wholeheartedly fulfilled the responsibilities in connection with the new situation, despite the sufferings and hardships they entailed, is a strong indication that she was aware of their significance.

An incident recorded by Nabíl-i-A'ẓam in His Narrative indicates that Ásíyih Khánum was aware of the identity and needs of at least some of the people who frequented Bahá'u'lláh's house. The same record reveals the fact that Ásíyih Khánum was familiar with the preparation of home remedies:

One day Mírzá Aḥmad conducted me (Nabíl) to the House of Bahá'u'lláh, whose wife, the Varaqatu'l-'Ulyá, the mother of the Most Great Branch, had already healed my eyes with an ointment which she herself had prepared and sent to me by this same Mírzá Aḥmad. The first one I met in that house was that same beloved Son of hers, who was then a child of six . . .[15]

The second surviving child born to Ásíyih Khánum was a daughter named Fáṭimih. She was born in 1846. Later Bahá'u'lláh gave her the appellation of Bahá'íyyih, and honoured her with the title of 'The Greatest Holy Leaf'. He also bestowed upon her the station of the most outstanding heroine of the Bahá'í Dispensation. The third child was born in 1849 and was named Mírzá Mihdí. He was later entitled the Purest Branch by Bahá'u'lláh.

THE MOST EXALTED LEAF

For a period of fourteen years, i.e. from the time of her marriage in 1835 until 1849, Ásíyih Khánum was Bahá'u'lláh's only life partner. During this time her lifestyle underwent drastic changes. She started off her married life with all the luxuries that people of her social standing enjoyed: position, wealth, comfort. She witnessed the adverse events and hardships which struck her father-in-law Mírzá Buzurg during the last years of his life. These developments must have affected her as deeply as they affected Bahá'u'lláh, her Husband, in shouldering responsibility for the members of the family and caring for their daily needs. She then saw the feverish activities of the Bábí community and shared the persecutions that Bahá'u'lláh suffered by virtue of His position as the leader of that community. Her substantial dowry was plundered along with Bahá'u'lláh's other belongings. Although these developments were rapid and harsh, Ásíyih Khánum faced them with remarkable equanimity. Her confidence in Bahá'u'lláh's wisdom and ability to deal with any and all eventualities was, no doubt, the most important contributing factor; another important one was the extraordinary capacity with which her Creator had endowed her, a capacity which helped her to recognize her blessings in life. That same capacity also enabled her to share all the sufferings and ordeals that fell to be the lot of her Husband.

ÁSÍYIH KHÁNUM

Bahá'u'lláh's second marriage took place in 1849,* when events of far-reaching significance with regard to the Bábí Faith were in the making. It was then, in May 1849, that the Shaykh Ṭabarsí upheaval came to an end. Bahá'u'lláh had tried to join the defenders of the fort, but He was arrested, imprisoned and bastinadoed in Ámul. A few months later Ṭihrán witnessed the martyrdom of seven prominent Bábís, the agitations in Nayríz and Zanján reached their peak, and in July 1850 the Báb Himself was martyred. Following the Báb's martyrdom, Bahá'u'lláh left Iran, at the request of Mírzá Taqí Khán, the Prime Minister, for Iraq. His journey took about a year. He visited Kirmánsháh on the way, where Nabíl-i-A'ẓam and Mullá 'Abdu'l-Karím-i-Qazvíní, also known as Mírzá Aḥmad, attained His presence.

During His absence from the capital, Ásíyih Khánum and her children lived in Mázindarán, i.e. Tákur and Yálrúd, near her family. This is discernible from the following statement by Nabíl:

* He married Fáṭimih Khánum, His paternal cousin, who had been married and widowed five years earlier (see p. 14). She was then twenty-one years old and had no children of her first marriage. Although the circumstances surrounding this marriage at a time when Bahá'u'lláh was beset by difficulties and uncertainties are not clear, there seem to have been certain considerations that made it necessary. Fáṭimih Khánum accompanied Bahá'u'lláh and His Family on their exile from Ṭihrán to Baghdad. She later returned to Iran, but rejoined Bahá'u'lláh around 1860. She bore several children. Her eldest son Mírzá Muḥammad-'Alí, known as the Greater Branch, broke his Father's Covenant and arose against 'Abdu'l-Bahá. She and her other children supported him and lost their heritage. She died in 1904.

THE MOST EXALTED LEAF

Ere Bahá'u'lláh's departure from Kirmánsháh, He summoned Mírzá Aḥmad and me to His presence and bade us depart for Ṭihrán . . . Mírzá Aḥmad was instructed to remain in Ṭihrán until His arrival, and was entrusted with a box of sweetmeats and a letter addressed to Áqáy-i-Kalím, who was to forward the gift to Mázindarán, where the Most Great Branch and His mother were residing.[16]

Three months after Bahá'u'lláh's return from Karbilá, hardships reached their climax when three Bábí youth made the attempt on the life of Náṣiri'd-Dín Sháh. This tragedy resulted in Bahá'u'lláh's imprisonment in the Síyáh-Chál of Ṭihrán in August 1852. When Bahá'u'llah arrived in the capital in May 1852, His family were probably still in Mázindarán. Upon arrival, He was welcomed by Ja'far-Qulí Khán, the brother of the Prime Minister, Áqá Khán-i-Núrí, and was His honoured guest for one month. He remained there until His departure for Shimírán. Thence he proceeded to Lavásán where He spent a month in Afchih. He may have been on His way to rejoin His family when soldiers, despatched by the government, took Him captive in Níyávarán. Bahá'íyyih Khánum, who was six years old when Her Father was arrested, related her recollections many years later.

My father was away at his country house in the village of (Níyávarán), which was his property . . .

ÁSÍYIH KHÁNUM

Suddenly and hurriedly a servant came rushing in great distress to my mother. 'The master, the master, he is arrested – I have seen him! He has walked many miles! Oh, they have beaten him! They say he has suffered the torture of the bastinado! His feet are bleeding! He has no shoes on! His turban has gone! His clothes are torn! There are chains upon his neck!'

My poor mother's face grew whiter and whiter. We children were terribly frightened and could only weep bitterly.

Immediately everybody, all our relations and friends, and servants fled from our house in terror, only one manservant, Isfandíyár, remained, and one woman. Our palace, and the smaller houses belonging to it were very soon stripped of everything; furniture, treasures, all were stolen by the people.[17]

To protect Isfandíyár from the wrath of the enemies, and to forestall any unforeseen consequences that his arrest might have entailed for Bahá'u'lláh, Ásíyih Khánum sent him away to Mázindarán.*

The conditions of life during this time became very difficult. Ásíyih Khánum rented a little house in an obscure quarter of the city and moved there with her children, after their magnificent house had been pillaged. While living there, they were in need of the barest necessities of life. One day, despite the

---

* Isfandíyár returned to Ṭihrán after a while to take care of the debts that his purchases for the family had entailed. Thereafter he returned to Mázindarán. (See A. Afnán, *Black Pearls*, Kalimát Press, 1988, pp. 29–30).

grave dangers facing her Son, Who was then about nine years old, Ásíyih Khánum was forced to send Him to seek help from His aunt, who lived in another part of the city. 'Abdu'l-Bahá made mention in His utterances in the West of an episode that occurred then:

I was a Child about nine years old when we were surrounded by calamities and assaulted by the enemies. They had thrown so many stones into our house that it was full of stones. We had nobody except Mother, sister, and Áqá Mírzá Qulí.* To provide us with better protection, Mother took us from the Gate of Shimírán to the Sanglaj Location, where she found a house in an obscure lane and she looked after us there. She strictly forbade us to leave the house until one day our living circumstances became so difficult that Mother told Me to go to My aunt's (Bahá'u'lláh's sister) house and tell her to use all means at her disposal to find us a few 'qirán'.†

My aunt's house was in the Takiyih of Hájí Rajab-'Alí, close to which lived Mírzá Hasan-i-Kaj Damágh. I went. The aunt tried very hard until she found five 'qirán', which she tied securely in the corner of a handkerchief, and gave to Me.

On My return, in the Takiyih, the son of Mírzá Hasan-i-Kaj Damágh recognized Me and immediately proclaimed Me as a Bábí. The children ran after Me.

---

* Mírzá Muhammad-Qulí, Bahá'u'lláh's youngest half-brother. When Mírzá Buzurg died he was an infant and was raised in Bahá'u'lláh's care. He accompanied Him on His exiles.
† Monetary unit in Iran known also as Rial.

The house of Ḥájí Mullá Jaʿfar-i-Istarábádí was near. When I reached there, I took shelter in the entrance area of the house. The son of Ḥájí Mullá Jaʿfar saw Me, but he neither prevented Me, nor did he disperse the children. I stayed there until it was dark. When I left that place, again the children pursued Me. They shouted and threw stones. When I reached the shop of Áqá Muḥammad-Ḥasan-i Sandúqdár, the children did not come any closer.

In brief, when I reached home, I was so tired and fearful that I collapsed. Mother asked, 'What is the matter with you?' But I could not respond. I passed out suddenly. Mother took the handkerchief containing the money and put Me to sleep.[18]

And again in connection with the same subject He says:

There was a time in Ṭihrán when we had every means of lifelihood and comfort, but they were all pillaged in one day. Life became so difficult that one day Mother put a little flour in My hand and I ate it like that.[19]

Bahá'íyyih Khánum's spoken chronicle provides further details about those days of calamity and peril:

The prison into which my father had been cast was a terrible place, seven steps below the ground; it was ankle-deep in filth, infested with horrible vermin, and of indescribable loathsomeness. Added to this, there was no glimmer of light in that noisome place . . . My noble father was hurled into this black hole, loaded with heavy chains . . . and here he remained for four months . . . No food was provided and it was with the utmost difficulty that my mother was able to arrange to get any food or drink taken into that ghastly prison.

When religious fanaticism was aroused against a person or persons, who were accused of being infidels, as was now the case with the Bábís, it was customary not simply to condemn them to death and have them executed by the State executioner, but to hand the victims over to various classes of the populace.[20]

She then explains how the butchers, shoemakers, blacksmiths and others were given the opportunity to carry out 'their pitiless inventions on the Bábís'. And as they were busy inflicting injuries upon the victim, 'a drum was loudly beaten' and the mob crowded to witness the scene. She continues:

These horrible sounds I well remember, as we three children clung to our mother, she not knowing whether the victim was her own adored husband. She could not find out whether he was still alive or not until late at night, or very early in the morning, when she determined to venture out, in defiance of the danger to herself and to us, for neither women nor children were spared.

How well I remember cowering in the dark, with my little brother, Mírzá Mihdí, the Purest Branch, at that time two years old, in my arms, which were not very strong, as I was only six. I was shivering with terror, for I knew of some of the horrible things that were happening, and was aware that they might have seized even my mother.

So I waited and waited until she should come back. Then Mírzá Músá, my uncle, who was in hiding, would

ÁSÍYIH KHÁNUM

venture in to hear what tidings my mother had been able to gather. My brother 'Abbás usually went with her on these sorrowful errands.

We listened eagerly to the accounts she gave to my uncle. This information came through the kindness of a sister of my grandfather, who was married to Mírzá Yúsif, a Russian subject, and a friend of the Russian Consul in Ṭihrán. This gentleman, my great-uncle by marriage, used to attend the courts to find out some particulars as to the victims chosen for execution day by day, and thus was able to relieve to some extent my mother's overwhelming anxiety as these appalling days passed over us.

It was Mírzá Yúsif who was able to help my mother about getting food taken to my father, and who brought us to the two little rooms near the prison, where we stayed in close hiding. He had to be very careful in thus defying the authorities, although the danger in this case was mitigated by the fact of his being under the protection of the Russian Consulate, as a Russian subject.

Nobody at all, of all our friends and relations, dared to come to see my mother during these days of death, but the wife of Mírzá Yúsif, the aunt of my father.[21]

After giving an account of the circumstances which led to Bahá'u'lláh's release from the Síyáh-Chál, Bahá'íyyih Khánum relates the joy of His homecoming:

And so he came to our two little rooms. Oh, the joy of his presence! Oh, the horror of that dungeon, where he had passed those terrible four months . . . The glory had won so great a victory that the shame, and pain, and sorrow, and scorn were of comparatively no importance whatever!

Jamál-i-Mubárak had a marvellous divine experience whilst in that prison. We saw a new radiance seeming to enfold him like a shining vesture, its significance we were to learn years later. At that time we were only aware of the wonder of it, without understanding, or even being told the details of the sacred event. My mother did her best to nurse our beloved, that he might have some strength to set out upon that journey on which we were to start . . .

Now was a time of great difficulty. How could she prepare? The poor, dear lady sold almost all that remained of her marriage treasures, jewels, embroidered garments, and other belongings, for which she received about four hundred túmáns. With this money she was able to make some provision for the terrible journey.[22]

Ásíyih Khánum Accompanies Bahá'u'lláh on His Exile

Soon after Bahá'u'lláh's release from the Síyáh-Chál, He accepted banishment to Iraq and was sent to Baghdad, accompanied by several members of His family and a few others. They set out from Ṭihrán on 12 January 1853. Among the members of Bahá'u'lláh's family were Ásíyih Khánum and two children: their eldest son, 'Abdu'l-Bahá, and their daughter, Bahá'íyyih Khánum, who were about nine and six respectively. Mírzá Mihdí, who was about three years old, was left in Ṭihrán. The separation from him was very hard for Ásíyih Khánum to endure, but the long and arduous journey during the severe winter months would have endangered his life. It was therefore necessary for him to stay behind.

The journey lasted for three months. Bahá'u'lláh, in a prayer which describes the intense sufferings He endured in the Síyáh-Chál, makes reference to His banishment to Iraq soon after His release from imprisonment:

. . . Thy decree was irrevocably fixed, and Thy behest summoned this servant to depart out of Persia, accompanied by a number of frail-bodied men and children of tender age, at this time when the cold is so intense that one cannot even speak, and ice and snow so abundant that is impossible to move.[23]

The details of Ásíyih Khánum's journey from Ṭihrán to Baghdad during those winter months of 1853 are scanty. The exiles travelled by mule and passed through the mountain passes of western Iran and areas bordering Iraq. Information available gives us some idea of the appalling conditions endured by the exiles. What we know of Ásíyih Khánum's ordeals during that journey we owe to Bahá'íyyih Khánum, whose spoken chronicle has been recorded by Lady Blomfield in *The Chosen Highway*:

This journey was filled with indescribable difficulties. My mother had no experience, no servants, no provisions, and very little money left. My father was extremely ill, not having recovered from the ordeals of the torture and the prison. No one of all our friends and relations dared to come to our help, or even to say good-bye, but one old lady, the grandmother of Ásíyih Khánum.

Our faithful servant, Isfandíyár, and the one negro woman who did not fear to remain with us, did their best. But we three children were very young, my brother eight, and I six years old. Mírzá Mihdí, the 'Purest Branch', was very delicate, and my mother allowed herself to be persuaded to leave the little fellow, only two years old, with her grandmother, though the parting with him was very sad . . .

My poor mother! How she suffered on this journey, riding in a takht-i-raván,* borne on a jolting mule! And this took place only six weeks before her youngest son was born!

Never did she utter one word of complaint. She was always thinking of some kindness for somebody, and sympathy she gave unsparingly to all in their difficulties . . .

When we came to a city, my mother would take the clothes and wash them at the public baths; we also were able to have baths at those places. She would carry the cold, wet clothes away in her arms – drying them was an almost impossible task; her lovely hands, being unused to such coarse work, became very painful.[24]

---

* Takht-i-raván: a portable couch mounted on a mule, horse or camel. The English equivalent of this term is palanquin or litter.

ÁSÍYIH KHÁNUM

Bahá'íyyih Khánum then goes on to describe the little house which accommodated them upon arrival in Baghdad, and the difficulties facing the exiles, especially her mother:

When we first arrived there, we had a very little house,* consisting of my father's room, and another one which was my mother's, and in which were also my eldest brother, the baby, and myself.

When Arab ladies came to see us, this was the only reception room. These ladies came because they had been taught by Ṭáhirih, Qurratu'l-'Ayn, during her visit to Baghdad . . .

Ásíyih Khánum, my dear mother, was in delicate health, her strength was diminished by the hardships she had undergone, but she always worked beyond her force.

Sometimes my father himself helped in the cooking, as that hard work was too much for the dainty, refined, gentle lady. The hardships she had endured saddened the heart of her divine husband, who was also her beloved Lord. He gave this help both before his sojourn in the wilderness of Sulaymáníyyih, and after his return.[25]

Ásíyih Khánum's agonizing ordeals in Baghdad reached their climax when Bahá'u'lláh retreated to the mountains of Sulaymáníyyih.

Our grief was intense when my father left us. He told none of us either where he was going or when he would

---

* This must be the house of Ḥájí 'Alí Madad in the old city, a rented house into which Bahá'u'lláh and His family moved in early May 1853.

return . . . So we, my mother, my brother 'Abbás and I, clung together in our sorrow and anxiety.²⁶

The intrigues employed by Bahá'u'lláh's half-brother, Mírzá Yaḥyá known as Ṣubḥ-i-Azal, increased in His absence. Mírzá Yaḥyá, who was not among the exiles when Bahá'u'lláh left Ṭihrán, had joined Him of his own free will; he went to Baghdad in disguise some two months later, and further complicated the already difficult conditions of life for the family. He cherished in his heart and mind the desire to lead the Bábí Community, but he had neither the courage, nor the inner knowledge and wisdom, nor the substance required for such a position. However, Bahá'u'lláh, who had raised, nurtured, and protected him after their father's death in Iran, provided him with every opportunity to recognize the truth. Bahá'u'lláh's retreat to the mountains of Sulamáníyyih, so soon after His arrival in Baghdad, was yet another step intended to help Mírzá Yaḥyá realise the folly of his hopes, and to assist the members of the community to fix their gaze upon Him Whom God would make manifest. He left Baghdad on 10 April 1854, exactly one year after His arrival there. No one knew of His intended departure or destination. Ásíyih Khánum's agonizing concern for Bahá'u'lláh during His two years' absence was immense.

During the two years of His sojourn in Sulaymáníyyih, Mírzá Yaḥyá's unreasonable demands on the members of His family increased. His intense fear of persecution had made him cynical and suspicious; in order to protect his own interests and ensure his safety, he did not wish the members of Bahá'u'lláh's family to associate with anyone. At the same time, he expected them to provide the means of comfort for him and his several wives. His expectations and behaviour, which betrayed his inner weakness of character and selfishness, made life unbearable for Bahá'u'lláh's family, with whom he lived. The precious child* that Ásíyih Khánum had borne during her arduous exile journey and had given birth to soon after arrival in Baghdad, died during Bahá'u'lláh's absence. This tragic event broke the grieving heart of his sorely-tried mother. Mírzá Yaḥyá, who wished to remain undiscovered lest he become a target for retribution, did not allow the child a proper burial. The body was given to an anonymous person to bury.

During this time the darling baby brother, born after our arrival in Baghdad, became seriously ill. Our guest would not allow a doctor, or even any neighbour to come to our help. My mother was heart-broken when the little one died; even then we were not allowed to have anybody to prepare him for burial. The sweet body of our beautiful baby was given to a man, who

---

* Named 'Alí Muḥammad. It seems that another son had been born to Bahá'u'lláh and Ásíyih Khánum prior to the birth of Mírzá Mihdí, the Purest Branch. The name of that child, who died in infancy, was 'Alí Muḥammad; the name was later given to the child born in Baghdad. This was Ásíyih Khánum's last child.

took it away, and we never knew even where he was laid. I remember so clearly the sorrow of those days.[27]

The details of what Ásíyih Khánum went through during Bahá'u'lláh's retreat in Sulaymáníyyih have not been recorded, and are unclear. Shoghi Effendi, in his message in Persian of 25 December 1939, refers to the blame, dispraise and slander aimed at her by the people of envy during the two years that the Blessed Beauty spent in the mountains of Kurdistán. He also refers to the humiliation, cruelties, and transgressions that she suffered at the hands of the stirrers of mischief. His review of Ásíyih Khánum's sufferings during that period reminds the reader of the prophecy of the Prophet Isaiah about her:

For the Lord hath called thee as a woman forsaken and grieved in spirit, and a wife of youth, when thou wast refused, saith thy God. For a small moment have I forsaken thee; but with great mercies will I gather thee. In a little wrath I hid my face from thee for a moment; but with everlasting kindness will I have mercy on thee, saith the Lord thy Redeemer.[28]

It was during the early years in Baghdad (it is not known whether it was before or after the Sulaymáníyyih period) while 'Abdu'l-Bahá was 'still in His childhood', that He recognized 'the full glory of His Father's as yet unrevealed station, a recognition which had impelled Him to throw Himself at His feet and to spontaneously implore the privilege of laying down His life for His sake'.[29] Whether the immensity of this highly charged spiritual experience and the feelings of ecstasy surging in the soul of 'Abdu'l-Bahá in His tender years were contained and escaped the attention of His mother is left to the imagination of the reader. If she was unaware of their significance, how could she bear the events taking place in Baghdad, which weighed so heavily on her sorrowful heart? Could she have remained untouched by the numerous evidences pointing to Bahá'u'lláh's extraordinary personality and station? These are legitimate questions.

During Bahá'u'lláh's absence from Baghdad, His family moved to the house of Sulaymán-i-Ghannám 'known, at that time, as the house of Mírzá Músá, the Bábí, an extremely modest residence situated in the Karkh quarter, in the neighbourhood of the western bank of the river . . .' On this house Bahá'u'lláh later conferred 'the official designation of the Bayt-i-A'zam (the Most Great House) . . .'[30]

Bahá'u'lláh's return from Sulamáníyyih on 19 March 1856 was by far the most happy event in years experienced by Ásíyih Khánum and the members of His family. Another happy occurrence was the reunion of Ásíyih Khánum with her son Mírzá Mihdí, entitled the Purest Branch. He joined the exiles in Baghdad after Bahá'u'lláh's return from Sulaymáníyyih. A. Ishráq-Khávarí says the reunion took place about 1860. He accompanied

THE MOST EXALTED LEAF

Fáṭimih Khánum, Bahá'u'lláh's second wife, on her return to Baghdad.[31] If the date is accurate, Mírzá Mihdí rejoined his family after seven years' separation. The means of communication in those days was by messenger post and messages took months to reach their destination. The delicate child that Ásíyih Khánum had to leave behind was rarely able to receive news of his beloved parents. And now after such a long time he could be again in the loving arms of his mother and the members of his family. It was truly a joyous occasion for all concerned. Mírzá Mihdí shared to the end of his life the anguish and hardships of the life of banishment to which his Beloved Father and the rest of His family were subjected.

The authority and sovereignty of Bahá'u'lláh, upon His return from Sulaymáníyyih, became clearer day by day. His new residence became the focal centre of activity. Members of the Bábí community travelled from Persia to Baghdad to attain His presence and derive knowledge and wisdom from Him. Seekers of enlightenment thronged His abode. Ásíyih Khánum's life was again filled with tremendous activity; she had to oversee the work in a house which had become the focus of attention for both believers and seekers.

The evidences of Bahá'u'lláh's might and sovereignty provoked the animosity of the religious leaders in Baghdad, who demanded His further banishment. The Persian religious leader in Iraq,

Sha<u>yk</u>h 'Abdu'l-Ḥusayn, was behind the agitation. His manoeuvres caused the issue of the decree by the Ottoman authorities banishing Bahá'u'lláh farther away from Iran.

When Bahá'u'lláh received the order of further banishment, He, His family and companions were celebrating Naw-Rúz 1863 in the vicinity of Baghdad. In less than a month's time Bahá'u'lláh and the Holy Family would have to leave Baghdad not to return there again. Bahá'u'lláh and some of His companions arrived in the Garden of Najíb Pá<u>sh</u>á, designated by Him as the Garden of Riḍván, in the afternoon of 21 April 1863.* Ásíyih <u>Kh</u>ánum and other members of the family stayed behind to make preparations for the journey. They were to follow Him shortly, but were unable to do so due to the overflowing of the River Euphrates. It was on 29 April that they arrived in that Garden. On 2 May 1863, Bahá'u'lláh, His family, and His companions left the Garden of Riḍván on their way to Constantinople, where they remained for less than four months. It was in this capital city of the Ottoman Empire that Sulṭán 'Abdu'l-'Azíz issued his 'infamous edict' banishing the exiles 'suddenly and without any justification whatsoever, in the depth

---

* The twelve days that Baha'u'lláh spent in the Garden of Riḍván are associated with the Declaration of His Mission, and are designated as the Riḍván Festival or the King of Festivals. The 21st of April, the date of His arrival in the Garden, the 29th when His family joined Him, and the 2nd of May, the date of departure, are Holy Days during which work is suspended.

of winter, and in the most humiliating circumstances, to Adrianople, situated on the extremities of his empire'.³² According to Bahá'u'lláh's own testimony: 'They expelled Us from the city (Constantinople) with an abasement with which no abasement on earth can compare. Neither My family, nor those who accompanied Me had the necessary raiment to protect them from the cold in that freezing weather.'³³

By then the children whom Ásíyih Khánum had tended so lovingly during the first part of the exile had become beautiful youth; they helped with necessary travel arrangements and other work that needed the close attention of members of Bahá'u'lláh's family. 'Abdu'l-Bahá, the eldest Son, had the lion's share.

The journey from Constantinople to Adrianople was long and arduous. It took place at the beginning of a very severe winter, lasted twelve days and entailed tremendous hardship. Upon arrival, Bahá'u'lláh, His family and companions stayed in a caravanserai called Khán-i-'Arab. After three nights He and His family moved to a house in the Murádíyyih quarter of the city. It took several months before a well-situated and spacious house in the centre of the city could be found. It was called the House of Amru'lláh, it had andarúní (inner quarters) and bírúní (outer quarters). Although the family enjoyed relative comfort in this house, the trickery of internal agitators such as

ÁSÍYIH KHÁNUM

Siyyid Muḥammad-i-Iṣfahání and Mírzá Aḥmad-i-Káshání became increasingly evident. Moreover, Mírzá Yaḥyá began to show signs of defection. His heedless attitude towards Bahá'u'lláh and his incessant intrigues against Him became extreme. His treachery was the cause of untold suffering to Bahá'u'lláh and His family. When he recognized his inability to gain the esteem and allegiance of the followers of the Báb by legitimate means, his excessive passion for leadership prompted him to plan and commit the heinous act of poisoning Bahá'u'lláh. Although the scheme was unsuccessful in achieving the hoped-for result, it made Bahá'u'lláh very ill. The illness lasted for a month and increased tremendously the anguish of Ásíyih Khánum and other members of the family for His safety and well-being. After Bahá'u'lláh recovered, the effects of the poison He had consumed in the home of His treacherous half-brother remained to the end of His life. When Mírzá Yaḥyá's deeds betrayed his true intentions and proved his unsuitability for membership in the Community of the Greatest Name, the great separation took place. The wavering in heart were severely tested, but the sincere ones were distinguished. The malicious doings of Mírzá Yaḥyá and his accomplices thenceforth took place openly and shamelessly. At this time (March 1866) 'Bahá'u'lláh withdrew with His family to the House of Riḍá Big, which was rented by His order, and refused, for two months, to associate with either friend or stranger, including His own companions.'[34] The separation between Bahá'u'lláh and Mírzá Yaḥyá came as a blissful relief to Ásíyih Khánum who was extremely concerned about the threatening circumstances surrounding the life of her Husband. Shoghi Effendi, in his message in Persian of 25 December 1939, refers to the events that transpired in the Land of Mystery (Adrianople). He says these events shook the believers and made the countenances of the beauteous Branch (Mírzá Mihdí) and the Most Exalted Leaf (Ásíyih Khánum) to glow with ever-increasing brightness in the midst of all calamities.[35] Bahá'u'lláh and His family later moved back to the House of Amru'lláh for six months before moving to the House of 'Izzat Áqá, the last of their residences in Adrianople. Moving from residence to residence clearly had implications for Ásíyih Khánum. The responsibilities commensurate with her position as the lady of the household were great indeed. Except for the brief period of His withdrawal, Bahá'u'lláh received the friends regularly in the bírúní of His house, responded to their needs for guidance and answered their questions. The proclamation of His Divine Mission further increased the activities of the community, which naturally had an impact on Ásíyih Khánum and the work she performed.

These trying years in Adrianople were about five. On 12 August 1868 Bahá'u'lláh, His family

ÁSÍYIH KHÁNUM

and companions left this far corner of the European continent, entitled by Him the Remote Prison and the Land of Mystery, for the final place of their exile, the citadel of 'Akká. According to Shoghi Effendi, 'Suddenly, one morning, the house of Bahá'u'lláh was surrounded by soldiers, sentinels were posted at its gates. His followers were again summoned by the authorities, interrogated, and ordered to make ready for their departure. "The loved ones of God and His kindred," is Bahá'u'lláh's testimony in the Súriy-i-Ra'ís, "were left on the first night without food . . . The people surrounded the house, and Muslims and Christians wept over us . . ." '[36] The journey was arduous, the future unknown and the final place of exile notorious for its inhospitable climate and disagreeable conditions. In the words of Shoghi Effendi:

'Akká . . . had sunk, under the Turks, to the level of a penal colony . . . It was girt about by a double system of ramparts; was inhabited by a people whom Bahá'u'lláh stigmatized as 'the generation of vipers'; was devoid of any source of water within its gates; was flea-infested, damp and honey-combed with gloomy, filthy and tortuous. 'According to what they say,' the Supreme Pen has recorded in the Lawḥ-i-Sulṭán, 'it is the most desolate of the cities of the world, the most unsightly of them in appearance, the most detestable in climate, and the foulest in water. It is as though it were the metropolis of the owl.'[37]

The distance between Adrianople and Gallipoli was covered in five stages and took several days. After three days in Gallipoli the exiles left by an Austrian-Lloyd liner for Alexandria via Madellí and Smyrna (Izmir). In Alexandria they changed ship and set out by another Austrian-Lloyd for Haifa via Port-Sa'íd. The journey from Haifa to 'Akká was by sailing boat. Bahá'íyyih Khánum has described the vessel which carried the exiles to Haifa, and their arrival in 'Akká:

There was no place in which we could lie down in that vessel. There were also some Tartar passengers in the boat. To be near them was very uncomfortable; they were dirty beyond description.

Our lack of food had reduced us to a seriously weak state of health.

At length we arrived at Haifa, where we had to be carried ashore in chairs. Here we remained for a few hours. Now we embarked again for the last bit of our sea journey. The heat . . . was overpowering. We were put into a sailing boat. There being no wind, and no shelter from the burning rays of the sun, we spent eight hours of positive misery, and at last we had reached 'Akká, the end of our journey. The landing at this place was achieved with much difficulty; the ladies of our party were carried ashore.

All the townspeople had assembled to see the arrival of the prisoners. Having been told that we were infidels, criminals, and sowers of sedition, the attitude of the crowd was threatening. Their yelling of curses and

ÁSÍYIH KHÁNUM

execrations filled us with fresh misery. We were terrified of the unknown! We knew not what the fate of our party, the friends and ourselves would be.

We were taken to the old fortress of 'Akká, where we were crowded together. There was no air; a small quantity of very bad coarse bread was provided; we were unable to get fresh water to drink; our sufferings were not diminished. Then an epidemic of typhoid broke out. Nearly all became ill.[38]

The arrival of the exiles in the prison-city of 'Akká took place on 31 August 1868. Exhausted by a long and arduous journey, the travellers were greeted by a hostile and contemptuous population. Some had gathered to see 'The God of the Persians'. They had mocking glances and their language was derisory. The prisoners were accommodated in an army barracks which also served as a prison. The insanitary conditions and the inedible food made the prisoners ill. Ásíyih Khánum's accumulated sufferings through long years of exile were beginning to show their effect and had made her frail. The foul smell of their place of confinement was impossible to bear. Her beloved daughter, Bahá'íyyih Khánum, fainted before her eyes. Her precious Son, 'Abdu'l-Bahá, who had acted as a shield for His Father ever since the family had left Baghdad, had to tend the sick and look after their affairs. But He, too, fell ill and added to Ásíyih Khánum's anguish.

THE MOST EXALTED LEAF

The circumstances surrounding Bahá'u'lláh's last place of exile were woeful. He and His companions had been sent there to perish. They had been confined in a place where water and air were foul, food was scarce and living conditions unendurable. Some succumbed to their miserable circumstances and were even denied a proper burial. The friends who made their way with untold hardships from Iran to 'Akká to attain Bahá'u'lláh's presence were sent back without achieving their heart's desire. Nearly two years elapsed and no improvement was in sight. Ásíyih Khánum's greatest comfort and joy in those perilous days was her closeness to Bahá'u'lláh and her beloved children, who were all in their twenties. But it did not last. She was destined to witness the tragic death of her beloved son, Mírzá Mihdí, the youngest of her surviving children, entitled by Bahá'u'lláh the Purest Branch. He was the one she had left in Iran at the time of her banishment to Iraq. He was the one with whom she had been joyfully reunited in Baghdad, after several years of agonizing separation. He was the one to whose meekness everyone testified. He was then twenty-two years old. He fell through an unguarded skylight in the roof of the barracks, the only place the prisoners were allowed to visit, and died less than twenty-four hours after his fall.

The martyrdom of the Purest Branch dealt Ásíyih Khánum the hardest blow. The published accounts in English of this tragic incident do not

ÁSÍYIH KHÁNUM

depict in detail its devastating effect on her, nor do they reveal her unqualified acceptance of Bahá'u'lláh's decisive decree to offer him up for the quickening of mankind and its unification. To familiarize the reader with this aspect of Mírzá Mihdí's martyrdom, I will go into some detail explaining the circumstances which led to it and the developments thereafter, based on information provided in a booklet published in Persian on the occasion of the hundredth anniversary of his martyrdom.

Mírzá Mihdí was one of Bahá'u'lláh's amanuenses. On the afternoon of 21 June 1870 he presented himself to His Exalted Father and offered his services. Bahá'u'lláh advised him to go back on the roof of the barracks – he often used the roof for prayer and meditation – and continue his prayers. Mírzá Mihdí returned to the roof and, fully wrapt in his prayers and unaware of the world around him, he paced the area chanting verses from one of Bahá'u'lláh's famous odes known as 'Qaṣídiy-i-'Izz-i-Varqá'íyyih'.

> He was pacing the roof of the barracks in the twilight, wrapt in his customary devotions when he fell through the unguarded skylight onto a wooden crate, standing on the floor beneath, which pierced his ribs . . .[39]

> The terrifying sound of the fall echoed in the surrounding area . . . It was as if the day of resurrection had been renewed. The loving, frail and weeping

mother of the Purest Branch forced herself to the site where her beloved son was lying. As she beheld him soaked in blood. she gave an agonizing sigh and lost consciousness. The Purest Branch, despite his weakness and tormenting pain, took his mother in his arms.

After a while, the relatives and those who were present removed the Purest Branch and placed him in a bed. The Most Great Branch, 'Abdu'l-Bahá, attained the presence of Bahá'u'lláh and, prostrating Himself before His Exalted Father, implored Him with tearful eyes to bestow healing [upon His brother]. The Blessed Beauty responded thus: 'O My Most Mighty Branch, leave him to his Lord', i.e. leave his affairs to God, so that He may do as He please. The Greatest Branch bowed His Head in submission and directed others to be resigned to the Will of God.

Nabíl says that at that time Ásíyih Khánum, the grief-stricken mother of the Purest Branch, attained the presence of Bahá'u'lláh, prostrated herself at the Threshold of His Grandeur, and said: 'My Lord, I entreat Thee to accept from me this ransom.' The Blessed Beauty conferred His bountiful favours upon her and advised her to be patient. Ásíyih Khánum responded: 'Whatever is Thy good-pleasure, that indeed is my heart's desire and my best beloved . . .'[40]

Bahá'u'lláh, referring to the martyrdom of His son, says in a prayer:

I have, O my Lord, offered up that which Thou hast given Me, that Thy servants may be quickened, and all that dwell on earth be united.[41]

The body of the Purest Branch was washed in the barracks before the eyes of Bahá'u'lláh. The traditional restrictions on women compelled Ásíyih Khánum to remain on the upper floor of the barracks, where the family lived, and mourn the loss of her beloved son. Neither could she nor any other member of the family accompany the body on its journey to the Nabí Ṣálih cemetery in 'Akká where it was laid to rest. They were prisoners and could not leave the barracks. What went on in the heart and mind of Ásíyih Khánum during those trying hours are not recorded anywhere. All we know is that none of her numerous woes and sufferings compared in magnitude to the loss of her beautiful son in the prime of his age. We will see later how the remains of the mother and the son were transferred from the original graves to their permanent resting places on Mount Carmel, and their monuments built next to each other.

Soon after the martyrdom of the Purest Branch, the conditions of Bahá'u'lláh's confinement eased; the barracks were needed by the Government for other purposes. Bahá'u'lláh and His family moved to several temporary dwelling places before they settled in the House of 'Abbúd. During the seven years of Bahá'u'lláh's stay in this house several occurrences took place which had a bearing on Ásíyih Khánum's life.

Although Yaḥyá Azal did not accompany Bahá'u'lláh and other exiles to 'Akká – from

Adrianople he and his supporters were banished to Cyprus – his chief instigator, Siyyid Muḥammad Iṣfahání, and four other Azalís were sent with Bahá'u'lláh to 'Akká. These five sympathizers of Azal did everything in their power to undermine Bahá'u'lláh in His final place of exile. They served as spies, reported the movement of the pilgrims to the authorities, spread distorted information and incited the population against Bahá'u'lláh and His followers. Their misconduct was the cause of confusion and immense suffering. Bahá'u'lláh, as the contents of the Fire Tablet revealed at that time shows, was highly distressed. He withdrew from the community and refused to see anyone. His silence and isolation emboldened the stirrers of mischief; they used every means at their disposal to discredit Bahá'u'lláh and His companions. Some of Bahá'u'lláh's ardent lovers, who could no longer bear to see Him suffer in the hand of these few evil doers, decided to exterminate the mischief-makers even at the cost of endangering their spiritual lives, knowing full well that He could not possibly condone such an action and would be displeased with them. This incident occurred in 1872 and brought untold hardships to Bahá'u'lláh, His family and followers. Ásíyih Khánum witnessed with anxiety and concern the events which caused her beloved Husband so much sorrow and grief. She watched closely the arrival of the guards who took both Bahá'u'lláh and 'Abdu'l-Bahá away. She spent long terrifying hours awaiting eagerly news of her loved ones. Her relief and delight knew no bounds when Bahá'u'lláh returned to the house following the interrogation, and 'Abdu'l-Bahá was released after a few days' detention.

It was during Bahá'u'lláh's stay in the House of 'Abbúd that 'Abdu'l-Bahá's marriage took place. This was, no doubt, one of the happiest events in Ásíyih Khánum's life. Her beloved and only Son was twenty-nine years old when His bride arrived from Iran. Bahá'u'lláh had arranged for Fáṭimih Khánum, whom He entitled Munírih Khánum, to come to the Holy Land. She arrived towards the end of the same year that the Azalís had been murdered. Five months later, in March 1873, the marriage of the Most Great Branch to Munírih Khánum took place. Ásíyih Khánum, assisted by her beloved daughter Bahá'íyyih Khánum, made all the arrangements for the wedding. She witnessed the blessings Bahá'u'lláh showered upon her new daughter-in-law on the afternoon of the wedding day, the seventh day of the month of fasting.

The simple wedding ceremony materialized the highest wish of Ásíyih Khánum earthly life. She beheld with her own eyes that banishment and ordeals could not thwart God's purpose for mankind. 'Abdu'l-Bahá, the Centre of Bahá'u'lláh's Covenant, was happily married and, before long,

THE MOST EXALTED LEAF

His mother enjoyed the pleasure of having her grandchildren around.

With the arrival of Munírih Khánum, members of her family, with Bahá'u'lláh's permission, began to settle in the Holy Land. Notable among them were Shamsu'd-Duhá (Khurshíd Bagum),* her daughter, Fáṭimih Bagum,† and her two grandchildren. They transferred their residence from Iṣfahán to the Holy Land at Bahá'u'lláh's behest. Such settlements widened the circle of friends with whom Ásíyih Khánum could associate.

In 1878 'Abdu'l-Bahá visited Beirut at the invitation of Midḥat Páshá, its governor. This was 'Abdu'l-Bahá's first journey outside the confines of His place of exile, and the first time Ásíyih Khánum was ever separated from her beloved Son for a considerable period of time. Her sorrow was intense. Bahá'u'lláh has made reference in one of His Tablets to the sorrow felt in 'Akká after 'Abdu'l-Bahá left for Beirut:

Praise be to Him Who hath honoured the Land of Bá through the presence of Him round Whom all names revolve . . . Sorrow, thereby enveloped this Prison-city, whilst another land rejoiceth . . . We beseech God

---

* Shamsu'd-Duhá was a prominent believer in Iran. She was married to Mírzá Hádíy-i-Nahrí, Munírih Khánum's uncle. When in Karbilá, she was arrested and tortured in place of Ṭáhirih. For further information, see *Memorials of the Faithful*, pp. 175–190.
† Fáṭimih Bagum was the wife of the King of Martyrs. Her mother's teaching activities before and after her husband's martyrdom caused them untold suffering. They were called to the Holy Land because there was no peace and protection for them in their home country.

ÁSÍYIH KHÁNUM

– blessed and exalted be He – that He may honour us with meeting Him soon.[42]

Some of the letters 'Abdu'l-Bahá wrote to the members of His family during that journey contain the most affectionate references to His beloved mother. He always referred to her as 'Ḥaḍrat-i-Válidih' (her eminence, the Mother). Ásíyih Khánum addressed Him as 'Áqá Ján' (beloved Master).

Bahá'u'lláh left the House of 'Abbúd in 1878. When He transferred His residence to the Mansion of Mazra'ih and thereafter to the Mansion of Bahjí, Ásíyih Khánum remained in the House of 'Abbúd, where lived also 'Abdu'l-Bahá, Bahá'íyyih Khánum, 'Abdu'l-Bahá's wife Munírih Khánum, and their children. Although the distance between the House of 'Abbúd, the Mansion of Mazra'ih and the Mansion of Bahjí is short, the primitive means of travel made it difficult for the female members of the Family to visit Bahá'u'lláh frequently. It was particularly difficult for Ásíyih Khánum, because the accumulated sufferings of long years of banishment and imprisonment had made her frail and ill. Nevertheless, whenever the means were available and she felt well, she would visit Bahá'u'lláh. There were also times when Bahá'u'lláh visited her and the members of His family in 'Akká.

During the period when this distance caused temporary separation between them Bahá'u'lláh wrote often to Ásíyih Khánum. Some of His Tablets revealed in her honour or about her are placed in the International Archives Building.

The last sorrowful event in the life of Ásíyih Khánum occurred in September 1882. The widow of the Báb, Khadíjih Bagum, whose cherished wish had been to attain Bahá'u'lláh's presence in 'Akká, passed away in Shíráz soon after the marriage of Bahá'u'lláh's daughter to her nephew took place. Ḥájí Siyyid 'Alí, the nephew, had asked her to request Bahá'u'lláh's approval for him to marry one of His daughters. Khadíjih Bagum made the request through Munírih Khánum, who was her guest as she passed through Shíráz on her way to the Holy Land, and it had been arranged that she herself would travel to 'Akká with Ḥájí Siyyid 'Alí. However, Khadíjih Bagum's brother and nephew did not honour their promise; they travelled to the Holy Land and informed Khadíjih Bagum that their plans did not allow the fulfilment of their pledge. This caused Khadíjih Bagum immense sorrow; she could not travel alone, and now had no means of attaining the presence of Bahá'u'lláh. She became depressed, fell ill and died. The news of her death made the Blessed Beauty very sad. It also prevented Ásíyih Khánum from meeting the wife of the Herald, Who had sacrificed His life for her illustrious Husband.

The succession of heart-rending events and protracted sufferings sapped Ásíyih Khánum's energy.

ÁSÍYIH KHÁNUM

During the last years of her life she suffered from poor health. The exact nature of her illness is not known. When the end was near, Bahá'u'lláh visited her in the House of 'Abbúd. He was at her bedside when she breathed her last breath. The year was 1886. At her bedside were also 'Abdu'l-Bahá and the Greatest Holy Leaf, her beloved children.

In a Tablet of visitation revealed after her death, Bahá'u'lláh refers to this second sorrowful event – the first being the passing of Khadíjih Bagum – besetting the people of Bahá. He then testifies that Ásíyih Khánum attained His presence at daytime and in the night season, that she gazed upon His Countenance, circumambulated His Throne, gave ear to His Call, resided in His House, clung to the Cord of His Covenant, held fast the Hem of the Garment of His Generosity and Bounty, until the fatal event, recorded in the Book, struck and weakened her. He then bears witness that she endured all the hardships and sufferings that He bore, until she offered up her soul in His path before His Countenance.

Bahá'u'lláh then reassures Ásíyih Khánum of God's good-pleasure; He bears witness that she drank the choice wine of recognition from the chalice of Utterance, that she endured patiently in the path of her Lord, that she believed firmly in God, in His Books, His Prophets, and in all that has been sent down from the Heaven of His Will. He bids her rejoice in the highest Paradise for having been mentioned by the King of Names, and re-affirms that she attained unto all good, that God elevated her to a station round which circled every glory and high station. He addresses her as the Most Exalted Leaf, and confirms that the sorrow caused by her death changed the light of the day to the darkness of night, transformed joy to sadness, calmness to agitation, and that the whole world was overtaken by grief because of the bereavement of the One for Whom the Qá'im had sacrificed Himself. He then confirms that she was with Him at all times, that she fled her home in the land of Ṭá and went with Him to Baghdad, from Baghdad to the Land of Mystery, from there to the Most Great Prison. He then addresses the people of Bahá thus:

O faithful ones! should ye visit the resting-place of the Most Exalted Leaf, who hath ascended unto the Glorious Companion, stand ye and say: 'Salutation and blessing and glory upon thee, O Holy Leaf that hath sprung from the Divine Lote-Tree! I bear witness that thou hast believed in God and in His signs, and answered His Call, and turned unto Him, and held fast unto His cord, and clung to the hem of His grace, and fled thy home in His path, and chosen to live as a stranger, out of love for His presence and in thy longing to serve Him. May God have mercy upon him that draweth nigh unto thee, and remembereth thee through the things which My Pen hath voiced in this, the most great station. We pray God that He may forgive us, and forgive them that have turned unto thee, and grant their desires, and bestow upon them, through His wondrous grace, whatever be their wish. He, verily, is the Bountiful, the Generous. Praise be to God, He Who is the Desire of all worlds, and the Beloved of all who recognize Him.'[43]

Happy is the handmaid that hath mentioned thee, and sought thy good pleasure, and humbled herself before thee, and held fast unto the cord of thy love. Woe betide him that denieth thy exalted station, and things ordained for thee from God, the Lord of all names, and him that hath turned away from thee, and rejected thy station before God, the Lord of the mighty throne.[44]

The funeral of Ásíyih Khánum, unlike that of her son which had occurred sixteen years earlier, was held with the dignity that her position as Bahá'u'lláh's companion in every one of God's worlds required. According to H.M. Balyuzi, the author of *Bahá'u'lláh, the King of Glory*:

Notables of 'Akká, as well as Muslim and Christian divines, came to follow the funeral cortège which was preceded by muezzins and reciters of the Qur'án. Schoolchildren joined the procession chanting verses and poems expressing their grief. Overwhelming was the sorrow of 'Abdu'l-Bahá . . .[45]

The loftiness of Ásíyih Khánum's station is made very clear in the above quotations from Bahá'u'lláh's Tablets revealed in her honour. The warning given to those who deny her exalted station, turn away from her, and reject her station before God, is significant.

THE MOST EXALTED LEAF

Shoghi Effendi refers to Ásíyih Khánum as 'the most distinguished of all the people', 'the Shining Star of the Celestial Heaven', 'the Spiritual Mother of the people of Bahá', 'the Wronged Leaf' which hath sprung forth from 'the Tree of Faithfulness', the 'Precious nd Exalted Treasure and the keepsake of the Abhá Beauty', and that 'Brilliant Star of the Firmament of Faithfulness'.

The dearth of documented information about this historical figure of our Faith is regrettable. However, the Writings of Bahá'u'lláh and 'Abdu'l-Bahá, the utterances of 'Abdu'l-Bahá and the Greatest Holy Leaf, and the messages of Shoghi Effendi provide the needed spark to create in our heart the fire of longing to draw nearer to our Spiritual Mother, who was sorely tried all her life for no other reason than the fact that she had been chosen to be the consort of the Supreme Manifestation of God. The prophecy of Isaiah in the 54th Chapter of his book is an ancient testimony to Ásíyih Khánum's grandeur and uniqueness.

Enlarge the place of thy tent, and let them stretch forth the curtains of thine habitations: spare not, lengthen thy cords, and strengthen thy stakes; For thou shalt break forth on the right hand and on the left; and thy seed shall inherit the Gentiles, and make the desolate cities to be inhabited. Fear not; for thou shalt not be ashamed: neither be thou confounded; for thou shalt not be put to shame . . . For thy Maker is thine husband; the Lord of hosts is his name; and thy Redeemer the Holy

ÁSÍYIH KHÁNUM

One of Israel; the God of the whole earth shall he be called.

He then assures her;

For the mountains shall depart, and the hills be removed; but my kindness shall not depart from thee, neither shall the covenant of my peace be removed, saith the Lord that hath mercy on thee.

Thereafter he imparts a most wonderful glad tiding:

O thou afflicted, tossed with tempest, and not comforted, behold, I will lay thy stones with fair colours, and lay thy foundations with sapphires. And I will make thy windows of agates, and thy gates of carbuncles, and all thy borders of pleasant stones. And all thy children shall be taught of the Lord; and great shall be the peace of thy children. In righteousness shalt thou be established . . . whosoever shall gather together against thee shall fall for thy sake . . .[46]

'Abdu'l-Bahá has made it clear in one of His Tablets revealed in honour of one of the believers in the West that this chapter is about His mother, Ásíyih Khánum:

As to thy question concerning the 54th chapter of Isaiah: This chapter refers to the Most Exalted Leaf, the mother of 'Abdu'l-Bahá. As a proof to this it is said: 'For more are the children of the desolate, than the children of the married wife.' Reflect upon this statement and then upon the following: 'And thy seed shall

THE MOST EXALTED LEAF

inherit the Gentiles, and make the desolate cities to be inhabited.' And truly the humiliation and reproach which she suffered in the path of God is a fact which no one can refute. For the calamities and afflictions mentioned in the whole chapter are such afflictions which she suffered in the path of God, all of which she endured with patience and thanked God therefor and praised Him, because He had enabled her to endure afflictions for the sake of Bahá. During all this time, the men and women [Covenant-breakers] persecuted her in an incomparable manner, while she was patient, God-fearing, calm, humble, and contented through the favour of her Lord and by the bounty of her Creator.[47]

Bahá'u'lláh's Tablets addressed to Navváb, and those revealed in her honour, are many. Shoghi Effendi translated excerpts from some of these Tablets and included them in his message of 21 December 1939, which he sent to the Bahá'ís of North America on the occasion of the transfer of the remains of the Purest Branch and Ásíyih Khánum to Mount Carmel. The selected excerpts reveal Ásíyih Khánum's exalted station.

The first Spirit through which all spirits were revealed, and the first Light by which all lights shone forth, rest upon thee, O Most Exalted Leaf,* thou who hast been mentioned in the Crimson Book! Thou art the

---

* This title was first bestowed by Bahá'u'lláh upon Ásíyih Khánum. After her passing, He conferred the title upon Bahá'íyyih Khánum. To avoid confusion, Shoghi Effendi translated Ásíyih Khánum's title as 'the Most Exalted Leaf' and Bahá'íyyih Khánum's as 'the Greatest Holy Leaf'.

ÁSÍYIH KHÁNUM

one whom God created to arise and serve His own Self, and the Manifestation of His Cause, and the Day-Spring of His revelation, and the Dawning-Place of His signs, and the Source of His commandments; and Who so aided thee that thou didst turn with thy whole being unto Him, at a time when His servants and handmaidens had turned away from His Face . . . Happy art thou, O My handmaiden, and My Leaf, and the one mentioned in My Book, and inscribed by My Pen of Glory in My Scrolls and Tablets . . . Rejoice thou, at this moment, in the most exalted Station and the All-highest Paradise, and the Abhá Horizon, inasmuch as He Who is the Lord of Names hath remembered thee. We bear witness that thou didst attain unto all good, and that God hath so exalted thee, that all honor and glory circled around thee.

O Navváb! O Leaf that hath sprung from My Tree, and been My companion! My glory be upon thee, and My loving-kindness, and My mercy that hath surpassed all beings. We announce unto thee that which will gladden thine eye, and assure thy soul, and rejoice thine heart. Verily, thy Lord is the Compassionate, the All-Bountiful. God hath been and will be pleased with thee, and hath singled thee out for His own Self, and chosen thee from among His handmaidens to serve Him, and hath made thee the companion of His Person in the day-time and in the night-season.

Hear thou Me once again, God is well-pleased with thee, as a token of His grace and a sign of His mercy. He hath made thee to be His companion in every one of His worlds, and hath nourished thee with His meeting and presence, so long as His Name, and His remembrance, and His Kingdom, and His Empire shall endure. Happy is the handmaid that hath mentioned thee, and sought thy good-pleasure, and humbled herself before thee, and held fast unto the cord of thy love. Woe betide him that denieth thy exalted station, and the things ordained for thee from God, the Lord of all names, and him that hath turned away from thee, and rejected thy station before God, the Lord of the mighty throne.[48]

Ásíyih Khánum, according to her daughter Bahá'íyyih Khánum, was

tall, slender, graceful, eyes of dark blue – a pearl, a flower amongst women. I have been told that even when very young, her wisdom and intelligence were remarkable. I always think of her in those earliest days of my memory as queenly in her dignity and loveliness, full of consideration for everybody, gentle, of a marvellous unselfishness, no action of hers ever failed to show the loving-kindness of her pure heart; her very presence seemed to make an atmosphere of love and happiness wherever she came, enfolding all comers in the fragrance of gentle courtesy.[49]

Her grand-daughter Ṭúbá Khánum has described her and her room in the House of 'Abbúd:

Her tiny room was simple and bare – the narrow, white bed, which was also the divan in the daytime; a very small table, on which was her prayer and other holy books, her 'qalam-dán' (pen case), and leaflets for writing; there was also her rosary, sometimes a flower

ÁSÍYIH KHÁNUM

in a pot, and lastly an old painted box holding her other frock and her other under-garment.

My eyes will always see her in her blue dress, with a white 'niqáb' on her head, and little black slippers on her tiny feet. Her sweet, smiling face, and her wrapt expression, as she chanted prayers in her musical voice.[50]

In December 1939, after the lapse of fifty-three years since Ásíyih Khánum's passing, the Guardian of the Cause of God, Shoghi Effendi, her great-grandson, transferred her remains and those of her son the Purest Branch to the slopes of Mount Carmel, despite strong opposition from the Covenant-breakers. He then announced the news of this joyous tiding in his message of 5 December 1939 to the American National Spiritual Assembly:

BLESSED REMAINS PUREST BRANCH AND MASTER'S MOTHER SAFELY TRANSFERRED HALLOWED PRECINCTS SHRINES MOUNT CARMEL. LONG INFLICTED HUMILIATION WIPED AWAY. MACHINATIONS COVENANT-BREAKERS FRUSTRATE PLAN DEFEATED. CHERISHED WISH GREATEST HOLY LEAF FULFILLED. SISTER BROTHER MOTHER WIFE. 'ABDU'L-BAHÁ REUNITED ONE SPOT DESIGNED CONSTITUTE FOCAL CENTRE BAHÁ'Í ADMINISTRATIVE INSTITUTIONS AT FAITH'S WORLD CENTRE. SHARE JOYFUL NEWS ENTIRE BODY AMERICAN BELIEVERS.[51]

And in his message of 21 December 1939 he referred to the 'capital institutional significance' of the transfer of the 'sacred remains':

ÁSÍYIH KHÁNUM

The transfer of the sacred remains of the brother and mother of our Lord and Master 'Abdu'l-Bahá to Mount Carmel and their final interment within the hallowed precincts of the Shrine of the Báb, and in the immediate neighbourhood of the resting place of the Greatest Holy Leaf, constitute, apart from their historic associations and the tender sentiments they arouse, events of such capital institutional significance as only future happenings, steadily and mysteriously unfolding at the world center of our Faith, can adequately demonstrate.[52]

Amatu'l-Bahá Rúḥíyyih Khánum, who was an eyewitness, has recorded the details of the transfer in *The Priceless Pearl*. She has also explained the reason for it:

> It had long been the desire of the Greatest Holy Leaf to lie near her mother, who was buried in Akka, as was her brother, Mihdi. But when Bahíyyih Khánum passed away in 1932 she had been befittingly interred on Mt. Carmel near the Shrine of the Báb. Shoghi Effendi conceived the idea of transferring the remains of her mother and brother, so unsuitably buried in Akka, to the vicinity of her resting-place and in 1939 he ordered in Italy twin marble monuments, similar in style to the one he had erected over her own grave. Fortunately these reached Haifa safely in spite of the war. Far from being a simple procedure, 'the consummation of this long, this profoundly cherished hope' proved to be extremely difficult . . . Whilst their tombs were still in process of excavation from the solid rock of the mountain, the Guardian had learned that the Covenant-breakers were protesting against the right of the Bahá'ís

THE MOST EXALTED LEAF

to remove the mother and brother of 'Abdu'l-Bahá to new graves, actually having the temerity to represent to the government their so-called claims as relatives of the deceased. As soon, however, as the civil authorities had the true state of facts made clear to them – that these same relatives had been the arch-enemies of the Master and His family, had left the true Cause of Bahá'u'lláh to follow their own devices, and had been denounced by 'Abdu'l-Bahá in His Will and Testament – they approved the plan of the Guardian and immediately issued the necessary papers for the exhumation of the bodies. Without risking further delay Shoghi Effendi, two days later, himself removed the Purest Branch and his mother to Mount Carmel.

After daybreak, accompanied by a few Bahá'ís, Shoghi Effendi went to Akka, opened one grave after the other, and brought the remains to Haifa . . . When the earth was removed from the coffin of the Master's mother he discovered the wood was still intact,* except for the bottom which had rotted away, and so he instructed them to gently remove the top. He told me the figure of 'Abdu'l-Bahá's mother, wound in her shroud, lay there so clearly outlined that one could almost discern her features, but it collapsed in dust and bones at the first touch. He descended into the grave and with his own hands helped to place the skeleton in the new coffin prepared for it; this was then closed, loaded on a waiting vehicle, and they all proceeded to the second Arab cemetery where the Purest Branch was buried and there opened his grave. As he had been buried two decades longer than his mother, and the

* The original coffin has been preserved

ÁSÍYIH KHÁNUM

interment had been hastily carried out in the days when Bahá'u'lláh was so strictly confined in the prison barracks of Akka, the coffin had entirely disintegrated and Shoghi Effendi again gathered up himself the few bones and dust that remained and again placed them himself in the second coffin that lay beside the grave to receive them . . .[53]

The coffins were then brought to Haifa by car. Shoghi Effendi and a few trusted servants of the Cause bore the coffins over their shoulders and carried them from the street up to a building adjacent to the resting place of Bahá'íyyih Khánum. The coffins were deposited in a room in this building for three weeks.

And now, again on the shoulder of the Guardian, they are borne forth to lie in state in the Holy tomb of the Báb. Side by side, far greater than the great of this world, they lie by that sacred threshold, facing Bahjí, with candles burning at their heads and flowers before their feet . . . The following sunset we gather once again in that Holy Shrine . . . Slowly, held aloft on the hands of the faithful, led by Shoghi Effendi, who never relinquishes his precious burden . . . Once they circumambulate the Shrines, the coffin of beloved Mihdí, supported by the Guardian, followed by that of the Master's mother, passes us slowly by. Around the Shrine, onward through the lighted garden, down the white path, out onto the moonlit road, that solemn procession passes. High, seeming to move of themselves, above the heads of those following, the coffins wend their way . . . They pass before us, outlined against the night sky . . . They approach, the face of the Guardian close to that priceless burden he bears. They pass on toward the waiting vaults. Now they lay the Purest Branch to rest. Shoghi Effendi himself enters the carpeted vault and gently eases the coffin to its preordained place. He himself strews it with flowers, his hands the last to caress it. The mother of the Master is then placed in the same manner by the Guardian in the neighbouring vault . . . Masons are called to seal the tombs . . . Flowers are heaped upon the vaults and the Guardian sprinkles a vial of attar of rose upon them . . . And now the voice of Shoghi Effendi is raised as he chants those Tablets revealed by Bahá'u'lláh and destined by Him to be read at their graves.[54]

When the entombment of the remains was successfully accomplished, Shoghi Effendi cabled on 26 December:

CHRISTMAS EVE BELOVED REMAINS PUREST BRANCH AND MASTER'S MOTHER LAID IN STATE BÁB'S HOLY TOMB, CHRISTMAS DAY ENTRUSTED CARMEL'S SACRED SOIL. CEREMONY PRESENCE REPRESENTATIVES NEAR EASTERN BELIEVERS PROFOUNDLY MOVING. IMPELLED ASSOCIATE AMERICA'S MOMENTOUS SEVEN YEAR ENTERPRISE IMPERISHABLE MEMORY THESE TWO HOLY SOULS WHO NEXT TWIN FOUNDERS FAITH AND PERFECT EXAMPLAR TOWER TOGETHER WITH GREATEST HOLY LEAF ABOVE ENTIRE CONCOURSE FAITHFUL . . .[55]

Shoghi Effendi referred in his messages in English of 21 December 1939 and in Persian of 25 December the same year to the significance of the transfer of the remains of the Purest Branch and his mother, Ásíyih Khánum. In English he said:

The swiftness and suddenness with which so delicate and weighty an undertaking was conducted; the surmounting of various obstacles which the outbreak of war and its inevitable repercussions necessarily engendered; the success of the long-drawn-out negotiations which the solution of certain preliminary problems imposed; the execution of the plan in the face of the continued instability and persistent dangers following the fierce riots that so long and so violently rocked the Holy Land, and despite the smouldering fire of animosity kindled in the breasts of ecclesiastics and Covenant-breakers alike – all combined to demonstrate, afresh and with compelling power, the invincible might of the Cause of Bahá'u'lláh.

. . . Avenged, eternally safeguarded, befittingly glorified, they repose embosomed in the heart of Carmel, hidden beneath its sacred soil interred in one single spot, lying beneath the shadow of the twin holy Tombs, and facing across the bay, on an eminence of unequally loveliness and beauty, the silver-city of 'Akká, the Point of Adoration of the entire Bahá'í world, and the Door of Hope for all mankind. 'Haste thee, O Carmel!' thus proclaims the Pen of Bahá'u'lláh, 'for lo, the light of the countenance of God, the Ruler of the Kingdom of Names and Fashioner of the heavens, hath been lifted upon thee.' 'Rejoice, for God hath in this Day established upon thee His throne, hath made thee the dawning-place of His signs and the day-spring of the evidences of His Revelation.'[56]

THE MOST EXALTED LEAF

In Persian he said:

O loved ones of God, these two precious and most exalted treasures, these two keepsakes of the sacred Beauty of Abhá, have now been joined to the third trust from Him, that is, to the daughter of Bahá and His remnant, the token of the Master's Remembrance. Their resting-places are in one area, on an elevation close by the Spot round which do circle the Concourse on High, and facing the Qiblih of the people of Bahá – 'Akká, the resplendent city, and the sanctified, the luminous, the Most Holy Shrine . . . For joy, the Hill of God is stirred at so high an honour, and for this most great bestowal the mountain of the Lord is in rapture and ecstasy.[57]

Shoghi Effendi then links this remarkable event to the following excerpt in the Tablet of Carmel revealed by Bahá'u'lláh, and says:

These exalted words have been recorded in the Tablet of Carmel: '. . . Well is it with him that circleth around thee, that proclaimeth the revelation of thy glory, and recounteth that which the bounty of the Lord thy God hath showered upon thee . . .'[58]

And in connection with the same theme:

The conjunction of these three resting-places, under the shadow of the Báb's own Tomb, embosomed in the heart of Carmel, facing the snow-white city across the bay of 'Akká, the Qiblih of the Bahá'í world, set in a garden of exquisite beauty, reinforces, if we would correctly estimate its significance, the spiritual potencies

Focal Point of World Administrative Centre of Future Bahá'í Commonwealth

Shoghi Effendi made the monuments of these members of 'Abdu'l-Bahá's family the pivot of the Arc he created on Mount Carmel, destined to become the seat of world administrative institutions of the Faith:

It marks, too, a further milestone in the road leading eventually to the establishment of that permanent world Administrative Centre of the future Bahá'í Commonwealth, destined never to be separated from, and to function in the proximity of, the Spiritual Centre of that Faith, in a land already revered and held sacred alike by the adherents of three of the world's outstanding religious systems.[60]

And in his message to the friends in the West he emphasized the same theme:

. . . the conjunction of the resting-place of the Greatest Holy Leaf with those of her brother and mother incalculably reinforces the spiritual potencies of that consecrated Spot which, under the wings of the Báb's over-shadowing Sepulchre, and in the vicinity of the future Mashriqu'l-Adhkár, which will be reared on its flank, is destined to evolve into the focal centre of those world-shaking, world-embracing, world-directing administrative institutions, ordained by Bahá'u'lláh and anticipated by 'Abdu'l-Bahá, and which are to function in consonance with the principles that govern the twin institutions of the Guardianship and the Universal House of Justice. Then, and then only, will this momentous prophecy which illuminates the concluding passages of the Tablet of Carmel be fulfilled: 'Ere long will God sail His Ark upon thee (Carmel), and will manifest the people of Bahá who have been mentioned in the Book of Names.'

. . . the association of these three incomparably precious souls who, next to the three Central Figures of our Faith, tower in rank above the vast multitude of the heroes, Letters, martyrs, hands, teachers and administrators of the Cause of Bahá'u'lláh, in such a potentially powerful spiritual and administrative Centre, is in itself an event which will release forces that are bound to hasten the emergence in a land which, geographically, spiritually and administratively, constitutes the heart of the entire planet, of some of the brightest gems of that World Order now shaping in the womb of this travailing age.[61]

Shoghi Effendi's creative and unprecedented plan made it possible for the resting-places of the faithful and close relatives of the Founder of the Faith and of the Centre of His Covenant to be established in one spot on God's Holy Mountain. It is significant that three of the four buried in this spot are women. The Monument Gardens which house their resting-places are visited by Bahá'í pilgrims from all over the world. This is indeed unique in the annals of religion.

REFERENCES

1. Isaiah 54:3,5.
2. Shoghi Effendi, *Guidance for Today and Tomorrow* (London: Bahá'í Publishing Trust, 1953), p. 75.
3. ibid. p. 74.
4. ibid.
5. 'Abdu'l-Bahá, *Tablets of 'Abdu'l-Bahá* (New York: Bahá'í Publishing Committee, 1930), Vol. I, p. 218.
6. ibid. pp. 208–209.
7. Arbáb, F., *Akhtarán-i-Tábán* (Ṭihrán: Bahá'í Publishing Trust, 132 BE), p. 91.
8. Lady Blomfield, *The Chosen Highway* (Wilmette: Bahá'í Publishing Trust, 1967), p. 39.
9. ibid.
10. Balyuzi, H.M., *Bahá'u'lláh, The King of Glory* (Oxford: George Ronald, 1980), p. 21.
11. *The Chosen Highway*, p. 40.
12. 'Abdu'l-Bahá, *Memorials of the Faithful*, translated by M. Gail (Wilmette: Bahá'í Publishing Trust, 1971), p. 200.
13. *Bahá'u'lláh, The King of Glory*, p. 63.
14. Nabíl, *The Dawn-Breakers*, translated by Shoghi Effendi (Wilmette: Bahá'í Publishing Trust, 1974), p. 299.
15. ibid. pp. 440–441.

REFERENCES

16. ibid. p. 591.
17. *The Chosen Highway*, pp. 40–41.
18. Zarqání, M., *Badáyi'u'l-áthár* (Karímí Press, 1921), vol. 2, pp. 205–206.
19. ibid. p. 206.
20. *The Chosen Highway*, pp. 41–42.
21. ibid. pp. 42–43.
22. ibid. pp. 44–45.
23. Shoghi Effendi, God Passes By (Wilmette: Bahá'í Publishing Trust, 1987), p. 109.
24. *The Chosen Highway*, pp. 45–46.
25. ibid. p. 47.
26. ibid. p. 51.
27. ibid. pp. 51–52.
28. Isaiah 54:6–8.
29. Shoghi Effendi, God Passes By, p. 241.
30. ibid. pp. 129–130.
31. A.H. Ishráq-Khávarí, *Rahíq-i-Makhtúm* (Ṭihrán: Bahá'í Publishing Trust, 131 BE), vol. 2, pp. 200–201.
32. Shoghi Effendi, God Passes By, pp. 158–159.
33. ibid. p. 161.
34. *Bahá'u'lláh, The King of Glory*, p. 230.
35. Shoghi Effendi, *Tawqí'át-i-Mubárakih* (Ṭihrán: Bahá'í Publishing Trust, 129 BE), vol. 2, p. 299.
36. God Passes By, p. 179.
37. ibid. pp. 185–186.
38. *The Chosen Highway*, p. 66.
39. God Passes By, p. 188.
40. A.H. Ishráq-Khávarí, Ḥaḍrat-i-Ghuṣnu'lláhu'l-Athar (127 BE), pp. 9–14.
41. God Passes By, p. 188.
42. *Tablets of Bahá'u'lláh revealed after the Kitáb-i-Aqdas* (Haifa: Bahá'í World Centre, 1978), pp. 227–228.
43. *Guidance for Today and Tomorrow*, pp. 75–76.
44. ibid. p. 75.
45. *Bahá'u'lláh, The King of Glory*, p. 369.
46. Isaiah 54:11–15.

REFERENCES

47. *Guidance for Today and Tomorrow*, p. 76.
48. Shoghi Effendi, *Messages to America: Selected Letters and Cablegrams Addressed to the Bahá'ís of North America* (Wilmette: Bahá'í Publishing Committee, 1947), pp. 34–35.
49. *The Chosen Highway*, pp. 39–40.
50. ibid. pp. 93–94.
51. Bahíyyih <u>Kh</u>ánum, *The Greatest Holy Leaf* (Haifa: Bahá'í World Centre, 1982), pp. 60–61.
52. *Messages to America: Selected Letters and Cablegrams Addressed to the Bahá'ís of North America*, p. 31.
53. Rúhíyyih Rabbání, *The Priceless Pearl* (London: Bahá'í Publishing Trust, 1969), pp. 259–260.
54. ibid. pp. 262–263.
55. ibid. p. 262.
56. *Messages to America*, pp. 31–32.
57. Bahíyyih <u>Kh</u>ánum, *The Greatest Holy Leaf*, p. 61.
58. Continuation of Shoghi Effendi's message quoted in 57 (omitted in *Bahíyyih <u>Kh</u>ánum, The Greatest Holy Leaf*).
59. *God Passes By*, p. 348.
60. ibid.
61. *Messages to America: Selected Letters and Cablegrams Addressed to the Bahá'ís of North America*, pp. 32–33.

www.ingramcontent.com/pod-product-compliance
Lightning Source LLC
Chambersburg PA
CBHW032022040426
42448CB00006B/700